engage

Level 2

Workbook

Alistair McCallum

OXFORD
UNIVERSITY PRESS

Welcome back

1 **Match the words with the numbers.**

1	82		A	six hundred thirty-five
2	71		B	fourteen
3	635		C	eleven
4	820		D	one hundred seventy
5	11		E	forty
6	14		F	seventy-one
7	40		G	eighty-two
8	170		I	eight hundred twenty

2 **Write the dates.**

1 12/01 _December first_

2 3/3 _____

3 1/15 _____

4 6/30 _____

5 9/29 _____

3 **Fill in the blanks with the correct adjectives.**

1 Are you ____angry____?

2 We're _____!

3 I'm _____!

4 It's _____.

5 They're _____.

6 She's _____.

4 **What's on the table? Fill in the blanks with *some* or *any*.**

1 There is _some_ cheese.

   There isn't _____ ham.

2 There aren't _____ apples.

   There is _____ soda.

3 There are _____ oranges.

   There isn't _____ water.

5 Circle the correct word.

1 Give **I** / (**me**) that pen, please. **I** / **me** want to write a letter.
2 It's Jane's birthday. **She** / **her** is sixteen. This present is for **she** / **her**.
3 **We** / **us** are going to the movies. Come with **we** / **us**!
4 **They** / **them** play their instruments really well. Listen to **they** / **them**!

6 Correct the mistakes in the sentences.

1 Tom's hands are cold! He needs his ~~boots~~ *gloves*.

2 Look at this camera. It's big!

3 Yesterday Kara bought a new jacket.

4 Rui has a new surfboard. It's really short!

5 It's sunny today. They're wearing hats.

6 My bag's on the bed. It's next to my shorts.

7 Put the words in order. Complete the dialog.

Tina: Hi, Carlos. (1) _What are you doing_ (you / are / what / doing)?

Carlos: (2) _____ (sitting / am / I) on the beach. It's hot and sunny!

Tina: (3) _____ (having / you / are) lunch?

Carlos: No, I'm not. It's eleven o'clock, and (4) _____ (am / I / drinking) a soda.

Tina: (5) _____ (is / sitting / your sister) next to you?

Carlos: No, she isn't. (6) _____ (is / swimming / she) in the sea.

8 Write negative sentences (✗), affirmative sentences (✔) or questions (?). Use the simple present.

1 my sister / like / basketball ✗
   My sister doesn't like basketball .

2 you / live / in London?
   _____?

3 my dad / work / at the supermarket ✔
   _____.

4 I / go to school / on Sundays ✗
   _____.

5 when / your brother / get up?
   _____?

6 My friend / play / the guitar ✔
   _____.

7 My parents / like / rock music ✗
   _____.

Unit 1

Vocabulary

1 Complete the puzzle with the activities.

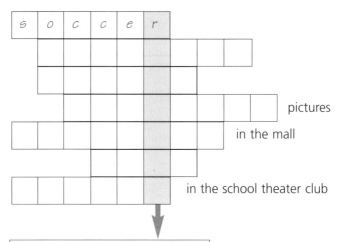

1 playing — s o c c e r
2 working on my
3 scuba
4 _____ pictures
5 _____ in the mall
6 playing the guitar in a
7 _____ in the school theater club

What's the mystery word? _____

2 Write the names of the people.

Tim   Rik   Mel   Kim   Jack   Lily   Lee   Ray

1 "It's fun!" _Rik_
2 "It's awful!" _____
3 "It's interesting." _____
4 "It's boring!" _____
5 "It's awful!" _____
6 "It's exciting!" _____
7 "It's OK." _____
8 "It's fun!" _____

Extend your vocabulary

3 Fill in the blanks with the words below.

hiking   snorkeling   snowboarding   camping   rock climbing

1 _Snowboarding_ is exciting!
2 We like _____.
3 _____ is fun!
4 We hate _____!
5 _____ is cool!

Grammar

1 Write the *-ing* form of the verbs.

1 go   *going*   6 give   _____
2 sit   _____   7 live   _____
3 practice _____   8 look   _____
4 read   _____
5 run   _____

2 Circle the correct word.

1 My brother **enjoy** / **enjoys** singing.
2 **Play** / **Playing** soccer is fun.
3 **Do** / **Does** you enjoy painting?
4 My friends **don't** / **doesn't** like shopping.
5 I love **ride** / **riding** my bike around town.
6 **Do** / **Does** your mom like watching TV?

3 Complete the dialog using the words in parentheses.

Ricky: Hi, Eva. **(1)** *Do you like reading* ? (*you / like / read*)

Eva: Hello, Ricky. **(2)** I_____! (*love / read*) And I like movies.

Ricky: Me too. **(3)**_____ is fun. (*go to the movies*) I like TV, too. **(4)**_____ TV? (*you / like / watch*)

Eva: **(5)**_____ is OK. (*watch TV*) I like music, too. I **(6)**_____ the violin, but I'm not very good! (*enjoy / play*)

Ricky: Wow! The violin! I don't play an instrument, but I **(7)**_____ to music. (*enjoy / listen*)

Eva: My dad's a musician. He **(8)**_____ with his band. (*love / play*) He plays the saxophone.

Ricky: That's amazing! **(9)**_____ is really difficult! (*play / the saxophone*)

Eva: I know! He practices every evening. Mom **(10)**_____ to it! (*hate / listen*)

Vocabulary

1 Fill in the blanks with words (→ or ↓) from the wordsearch.

T	H	L	I	T	T	E	R	E	R	H
N	E	S	A	L	O	T	O	F	E	O
O	B	U	I	L	D	I	N	G	S	U
I	P	O	L	L	U	T	I	O	N	S
S	N	T	E	R	T	A	I	N	M	E
E	T	R	A	F	F	I	C	E	N	S
O	P	E	N	S	P	A	C	E	S	T

I live in a big city.

1 There's a lot of _t r a f f i c_.

2 There's a lot of _ _ _ _ _.

3 There's a lot of _ _ _ _ _ _ _ _ _.

4 There are a lot of _ _ _ _ _ _.

5 There are a lot of _ _ _ _ _ _ _ _ _.

6 There's a lot of _ _ _ _ _ _.

7 There aren't many _ _ _ _ _ _ _ _ _ _.

Use the other letters to complete the sentence.

8 I like my city because _there's_ _____.

2 Label the picture with the words below.

bridge   farmhouse   woods   field   fence   river

Grammar

1 Put the words in the correct column.

> cars   traffic   people   water   bottles   litter   students   money

Countable	Uncountable
cars	

2 Circle the correct word.

1 How **much** / **(many)** students are there in your class?

2 There's **a lot of** / **much** litter on the street.

3 How **much** / **many** water is there in that bottle?

4 I can't buy a new skateboard. I don't have **much** / **many** money!

5 This room is crowded. There are **a lot of** / **many** people here.

6 There aren't **much** / **many** open spaces near my house.

3 Write questions with *How much* or *How many* and *is there* or *are there*.

1   _How many_ movie theaters _are there_ in your town?

2 _____ traffic _____ in the street today?

3 _____ rooms _____ in your house?

4 _____ cans of soda _____ in the refrigerator?

5 _____ noise _____ in the classroom?

4 These sentences are wrong. Write the correct sentences.

1   There's a lot of coffee in the jar.
   There isn't _much_ coffee in the jar.

2   I have a lot of CDs.
   I don't have _____ CDs.

3   There are a lot of people in the movie theater.
   _____
   _____ .

4   We have a lot of food.
   _____
   _____ .

5   There's a lot of traffic in our town.
   _____ .

Unit 2

Vocabulary

1 **Fill in the blanks with the words below.**

> listen   go   play   watch   play   read   eat   go

1 On the weekend, I usually go to the sports club and _play_ basketball.

2 I don't watch TV much, but I _____ a lot of magazines.

3 I don't _____ to school on Sundays.

4 There's always a lot of noise in Serena's room. She _____s to loud music all the time!

5 In summer, we sometimes _____ climbing in the mountains.

6 Mom and dad usually _____ a movie on Friday nights.

7 My brother _____s the piano and the guitar.

8 On Saturdays, I usually meet my friends and we _____ fast food.

2 **Match the pictures with the sentences below.**

1 He's cooking a meal. _C_

2 They're sunbathing. ___

3 They're watching a comedy show. ___

4 She's playing baseball. ___

5 She's sending a text message. ___

6 He's fishing. ___

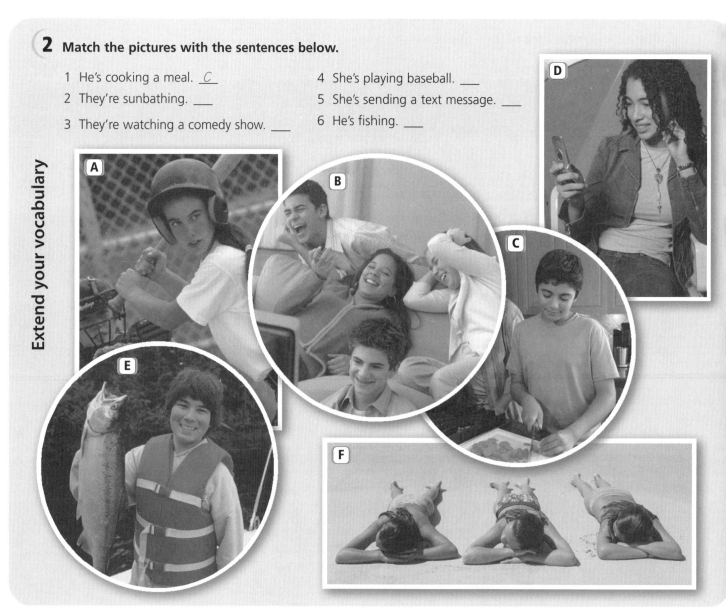

Extend your vocabulary

Grammar

1 Are these sentences about what's happening right now, or what usually happens? Check (✓) one box for each sentence.

	right now	usually
1 Slow down! You're driving too fast!	✓	
2 Wakako speaks Japanese.		
3 We're listening to a CD.		
4 Dad doesn't watch horror movies.		
5 We have lunch at 12 o'clock.		
6 Amy isn't wearing her new T-shirt.		
7 I don't listen to classical music.		
8 Ron isn't doing his homework.		

2 Circle the correct form of the verb.

1   I usually **get up** / **am getting up** at seven o'clock.
2   Right now, Katie **talks** / **is talking** to her friend on her cell phone.
3   My mom's a teacher. She **works** / **is working** at the University.
4   Carlos can't come to your house right now. He **has** / **is having** dinner.
5   My dad likes classical music. He **doesn't listen** / **isn't listening** to hip hop.
6   How do **you travel** / **are you traveling** to school every day?
7   Why do **you wear** / **are you wearing** gloves? It isn't cold today!

3 Fill in the blanks with the correct form of the verb.

Enzo is a soccer player. He (1) _____*plays*_____
(play) for Royal United. It's Saturday today. Enzo
usually (2) _____ (play) soccer on
Saturdays, but he (3) _____ (not
play) soccer today.
He's on holiday with his family. Right now he
(4) _____ (sunbathe). His children
(5) _____ (swim) in the pool. His
wife Ruby (6) _____ (listen) to
music. Enzo likes this hotel. He
(7) _____ (come) here with his
family every summer.

Right now

Vocabulary

1 Label the pictures with words from the word snake.

clothes grass dishes make garbage clean lunch take out table make room cut bed set wash put away

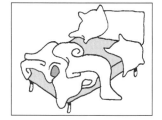

1 __make__
   the __bed__

2 _____
   _____

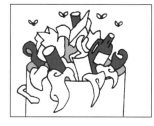

3 _____ _____
   the _____

4 _____
   the _____

5 _____
   the _____

6 _____
   the _____

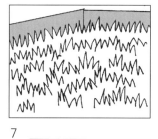

7 _____
   the _____

8 _____
   the _____

Extend your vocabulary

2 Fill in the blanks with the verbs below.

dust   polish   fix   do the laundry   sweep

1 He has to
   __fix__ his
   car.

2 She has to
   _____
   the floor.

3 He has to
   _____
   the boots.

4 He has to
   _____
   the furniture.

5 He has to _____
   _____.

Grammar

Chores for the weekend

	Tim	Tina	Mom	Dad
cut the grass		✔	✔	
wash the dishes		✔		✔
make lunch	✔	✔		✔
fix the car				✔
do the laundry	✔	✔		
make the beds			✔	✔
clean the kitchen	✔		✔	

1 Look at the chart. Circle the correct form of the verb.

1 Mom **have to /** **has to** cut the grass.
2 Tim and Tina **don't / doesn't** have to make their beds.
3 Mom **don't / doesn't** have to fix the car.
4 Tina and Dad **have to / has to** wash the dishes.
5 **Do / Does** Tina have to wash the dishes?

2 Who's speaking? Match the sentences with the people.

1 "We have to do the laundry."   A Dad
2 "I don't have to make lunch."   B Tim and Mom
3 "I have to fix the car."   C Tina
4 "I have to wash the dishes, but I   D Tina and Tim
    don't have to make the beds."   E Mom
5 "We don't have to wash the dishes."

3 Fill in the blanks with *have to*, *has to*, *don't have to* or *doesn't have to*.
Read Tim's email to his friends.

From: Tim
To: Mike
Subject: the weekend

Hi Mike
There's a lot to do this weekend! The car isn't working, so Dad (1) ___*has to*___ fix it.
Tina and I (2) _____ do the laundry, but we (3) _____ make our beds.
Mom (4) _____ cut the grass, because it's too long. Mom usually has to make
lunch, but she (5) _____ make lunch this weekend. Tina and Dad (6)
_____ wash the dishes. I (7) _____ wash the dishes, but I (8) _____
clean the kitchen with Mom. Everyone's going to be very busy!
See you soon,
Tim

11

Unit 3

Vocabulary

1 Unscramble the words in the sentences.

1 His hair is __*long*__ (glon)
  and _____ (ryulc).

2 She isn't _____ (hotrs).
  She's _____ (latl).

3 Her hair isn't _____ (tagirths).
  It's _____ (vywa).

4 His shirt isn't _____
  (hitgt). It's _____ (esolo).

5 Her shoes aren't _____ (wol).
  They're _____ (gihh).

2 Label the clothes with the correct adjectives.

| spotted | flowered | checked | plain | striped | patterned |

Extend your vocabulary

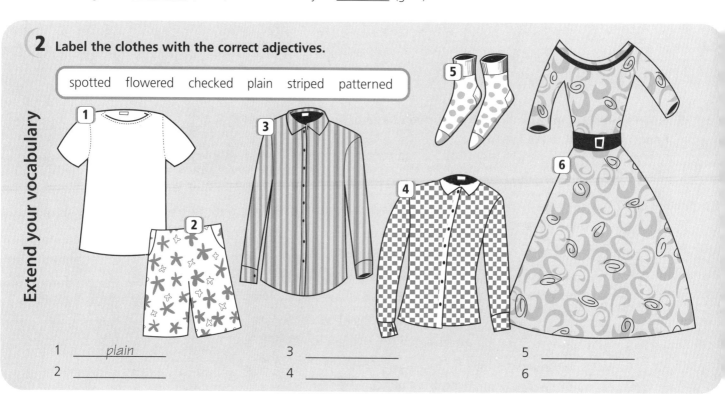

1 _____*plain*_____

2 _____

3 _____

4 _____

5 _____

6 _____

Grammar

1 Circle the correct comparative form of the adjectives.

1 big ➔ biger / (bigger)
2 short ➔ shorter / shortier
3 curly ➔ curlyer / curlier

4 good ➔ gooder / better
5 hot ➔ hotter / hoter
6 sad ➔ sader / sadder

2 Write the comparative form of the adjectives.

1 funny _funnier_
2 tight _____
3 fat _____

4 bad _____
5 loose _____
6 easy _____

3 Put the words in the correct order to make sentences.

1 bigger / is / London / than
   New York _is bigger than London_____.
2 tighter / my old jeans / than / are
   My new jeans _____.
3 is / Book 2 / than / easier
   Book 1 _____.
4 than / are / my classmates / noisier
   My sister's classmates _____.

4 Look at the pictures and write sentences about José and Pamela. Use the words in parentheses.

1 _Pamela is shorter than José_____. (Pamela / short / José)
2 _____. (José's jeans / tight / Pamela's jeans)
3 _____. (Pamela's room / clean / José's room)
4 _____. (José / slim / Pamela)
5 _____. (Pamela's hair / long / José's hair)

Vocabulary

1 Do the crossword.

Down

He loves playing the guitar and writing songs. He's _____.

2 She's kind, and often does things for people. She's _____.

Across

3 Her room is a mess, and her books and clothes are all over the floor. She's _____.

4 Those children are never quiet. They're _____.

5 He likes sport, but he doesn't like losing. He's _____.

6 She loves going to parties. She's _____.

```
1                              2
  c
3          r
           e
4          a
           t
5          i
           v
6          e
```

2 Read the descriptions, and write the correct adjective.

lazy   cheerful   reliable   shy   hardworking

1 Rita always arrives in class on time. She always does her homework. If she says she's going to do something, she does it! _reliable_

2 Matt likes watching TV and playing computer games, but he doesn't like doing his homework! _____

3 Ruby doesn't like meeting new people. She has some friends, but she doesn't like going to parties. _____

4 Roger always does well at school. He reads a lot, and asks a lot of questions. After school, he goes to the library to study! _____

5 Libby is always happy and talkative. She enjoys being with her friends. She smiles all the time! _____

Extend your vocabulary

Grammar

1 Circle the correct comparative form of the adjectives.

1 helpful → **helpfuller /(more helpful)**
2 cold → **colder / more cold**
3 sociable → **sociabler / more sociable**
4 difficult → **difficulter / more difficult**
5 thick → **thicker / more thick**
6 energetic → **energeticer / more energetic**
7 interesting → **interestinger / more interesting**
8 happy → **happier / more happy**

2 Look at the chart. Circle T (True) or F (False).

Ken

Tony

Sonja

We asked three teenagers about their character and appearance. Here are their answers.

Are you...	Ken	Sonja	Tony
... competitive?	•••	••	
... sociable?	•	••	•••
... lazy?	•	••	••
... helpful?	•	••	•••
... slim?	••	•••	•
... creative?	•	•••	••
... strong?	•••	••	•

1 Ken is more creative than Sonja. T /F
2 Sonja is stronger than Tony. T / F
3 Tony is more competitive than Ken. T / F
4 Sonja is more sociable than Tony. T / F
5 Tony is more helpful than Sonja. T / F
6 Ken is slimmer than Sonja. T / F

3 Write sentences about Ken, Sonja and Tony. Use the words in parentheses.

1 *Ken is more competitive than Tony*   . (Ken / competitive / Tony)
2 _____ . (Sonja / lazy / Ken)
3 _____ . (Tony / sociable / Ken)
4 _____ . (Sonja / slim / Tony)
5 _____ . (Sonja / creative / Ken)
6 _____ . (Ken / strong / Sonja)

Unit 4

Vocabulary

1 Circle nine adjectives about the weather in the wordsearch. Then write the words.

W	Q	V	H	C	E	R	C
U	O	C	O	L	D	Y	A
N	I	A	T	O	B	S	H
V	P	E	S	U	N	N	Y
O	W	I	N	D	Y	O	S
R	A	I	N	Y	I	W	E
T	R	K	E	I	C	Y	D
E	M	A	G	B	L	U	N

1 h _ot_____
2 c _____
3 w _____
4 r _____
5 i _____
6 w _____
7 s _____
8 c _____
9 s _____

2 Fill in the blanks with the words below.

flood   thunder   storm   power cut   lightning

1 Yesterday afternoon there was a terrible ___storm___.
The _____ was very loud!

2 We looked out of the window. There was a lot of
_____. It was scary.

3 It was very rainy, and there was a _____
near our house.

4 Then there was a _____ all night!

Grammar

1 **Circle the correct word(s).**

1 Where **was** / **were** you yesterday evening?
2 There **was** / **were** a storm last night.
3 Leila and I **wasn't** / **weren't** at school yesterday.
4 When **she was** / **was she** in England?
5 There **wasn't** / **weren't** any rain this morning.
6 I **was** / **were** at a party last Saturday.

2 **Look at Annie's blog. Fill in the blanks with** *was, were, wasn't* **or** *weren't.*

Annie's Holiday

Last summer I (1) ___was___ in a National Park in Kenya with my little brother Frank and my parents. There (2) _____ any hotels – we were in a small hut! The weather (3) _____ hot and dry, but it was cold at night.

There weren't many people in the Park. It (4) _____ crowded. But there (5) _____ a lot of interesting animals. There (6) _____ lions, elephants and snakes.

One night there (7) _____ an enormous spider in our hut. My brother was scared, but I (8) _____. It (9) _____ a beautiful spider!

3 **You are talking to Annie. Complete the dialog.**

You: Where were you last year?
Annie: I (1) _was_ in Kenya.
You: (2) _____ _____ rainy?
Annie: No, it wasn't. (3) _____ _____ hot and dry.
You: (4) _____ _____ any interesting animals?
Annie: Yes, (5) _____ _____. And one night (6) _____ _____ a big spider in our hut!
You: (7) _____ _____ scared?
Annie: No, (8) _____ _____. It (9) _____ a beautiful spider!

Vocabulary

1 Unscramble the verbs. Then write them in the puzzle.

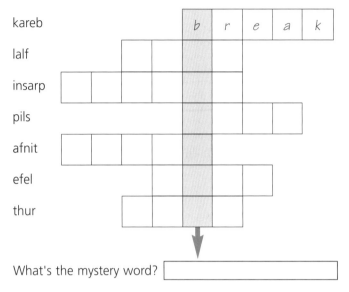

kareb

lalf

insarp

pils

afnit

efel

thur

| | | | | b | r | e | a | k |

What's the mystery word? _____

Extend your vocabulary

2 Fill in the blanks with the words below.

a temperature   a cold   a toothache   a headache   a sore throat

1 _____

2 _____

3 _____

4 _____

5 _____

Grammar

1 Check (✔) regular or irregular.

				regular	irregular
1	climb	→	climbed	✔	
2	feel	→	felt		
3	want	→	wanted		
4	meet	→	met		
5	celebrate	→	celebrated		
6	hurry	→	hurried		
7	eat	→	ate		
8	slip	→	slipped		
9	have	→	had		
10	buy	→	bought		

2 Fill in the blanks with the simple past of the verbs in parentheses. All the verbs are regular.

1 I __arrived__ (arrive) at school late this morning.

2 Graziella _____ (telephone) me at ten o'clock last night.

3 Tommy _____ (drop) a plate on the kitchen floor.

4 I _____ (visit) my grandparents last Sunday.

5 Dan _____ (carry) his suitcases to the station.

6 Sheila _____ (invite) me to her party.

3 Look at Miguel's diary for last week. Fill in the blanks with the simple past.

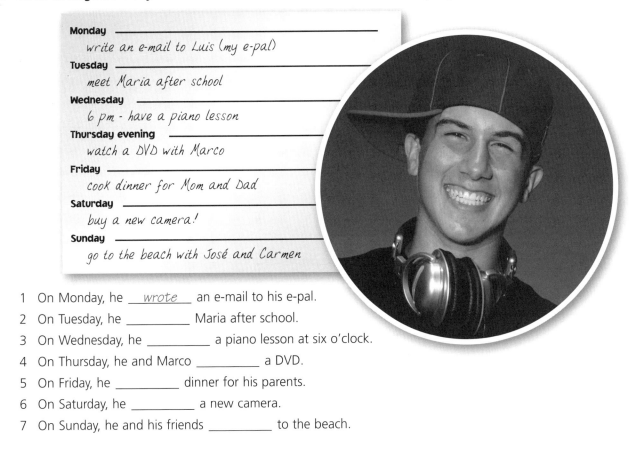

Monday _____
    write an e-mail to Luis (my e-pal)
Tuesday _____
    meet Maria after school
Wednesday _____
    6 pm - have a piano lesson
Thursday evening _____
    watch a DVD with Marco
Friday _____
    cook dinner for Mom and Dad
Saturday _____
    buy a new camera!
Sunday _____
    go to the beach with José and Carmen

1 On Monday, he __wrote__ an e-mail to his e-pal.

2 On Tuesday, he _____ Maria after school.

3 On Wednesday, he _____ a piano lesson at six o'clock.

4 On Thursday, he and Marco _____ a DVD.

5 On Friday, he _____ dinner for his parents.

6 On Saturday, he _____ a new camera.

7 On Sunday, he and his friends _____ to the beach.

Unit 5

Vocabulary

1 Do the crossword.

Down

1
2
3

Across

4

5

6

Across clue squares: 1 g u i t a r

2 Label the pictures with the words below.

> stage   orchestra   band   conductor   choir   loudspeakers   backing singers

Extend your vocabulary

A rock concert

1 *loudspeakers*
2 _____
3 _____
4 _____

A classical concert

5 _____
6 _____
7 _____

Grammar

Laura had a party at a restaurant. A lot of her classmates came to the party. They ate burgers and drank soda. Laura's parents gave her a new DVD player. She liked it!

Paul didn't have a party. He went to London with his parents. They stayed in a beautiful hotel and visited some interesting places. Paul liked London, but he didn't like the weather!

Daniel had a small party at home. His schoolmates didn't come, but all his family came. Daniel's dad played the guitar and sang. Daniel's mom cooked pizza. After the meal, they went into the garden and watched fireworks.

1 Read about the three birthdays. Write short answers.

1 Did Laura have a party? _Yes, she did_ .
2 Did Laura's parents give her a new skateboard? _____ .
3 Did Laura like her present? _____ .
4 Did Paul have a party? _____ .
5 Did Paul and his parents go to London? _____ .
6 Did Daniel's dad play the guitar? _____ .
7 Did Daniel's mom cook burgers? _____ .

2 Put the words in order to make questions. Then write short answers.

1 come / Laura's classmates / did / to her party?
   Did Laura's classmates _come to her party_ ? _Yes, they did_ .
2 did / pizza / Laura and her friends / eat?
   Did Laura and her friends _____ ? _____ .
3 to New York / go / Paul / did?
   _____ ? _____ .
4 stay / did / at a beautiful hotel / Paul and his parents?
   _____ ? _____ .
5 did / the piano / play / Daniel's dad?
   _____ ? _____ .

3 These sentences are wrong. Write correct sentences using *didn't*.

1 Laura had a party at home.
   No! She _____didn't have a party_____ at home.
2 Laura and her friends drank coffee.
   No! They _____ coffee.
3 Paul and his parents stayed at a friend's house.
   No! _____ .
4 Paul liked the weather in London.
   No! _____ .
5 Daniel had a big party.
   No! _____ .
6 Daniel and his family watched a movie.
   No! _____ .

Vocabulary

1 **Read about Olaf Jonsen. Then fill in the blanks with the words below.**

> signed a contract   won an award   grew up   recorded
> had a hit record   became famous   started his career

Olaf Jonsen was born on December 6th 1974. He (1) ___grew up___ in a small town in Norway. He (2) _____ as a singer in the school choir. He (3) _____ with a music company in 2002, and (4) _____ the album *Blue notes* in the same year. Olaf (5) _____ in 2004 when his second album *Finding my way* sold a million copies, and he (6) _____ with the song *New day*. In 2005 he (7) _____ for Best Male Songwriter at the European Music Festival.

2 **Fill in the blanks with the verbs and phrases below.**

> went to college   offered   had an interview   passed   graduated   applied for a job

Hi! My name's Terry Hardcastle. I'm a journalist, and I work at the Daily News.

1 I ___graduated___ from high school when I was 18.

2 I _____ and studied hard.

3 Four years later, I took my exams. They were difficult, but I _____!

4 I enjoy writing, so I _____ as a journalist.

5 Two weeks later, I _____ with the people at the newspaper. It was scary!

6 They _____ me the job. I was very happy. I started last week!

Extend your vocabulary

Grammar

1 **Match the questions with the answers.**

1 What did you buy?

2 Where did the children play soccer?

3 When did Karen move to London?

4 Why did Julio win the award?

5 How many goals did Ronaldo score?

6 How did you get to school today?

A In 2001.

B Three!

C On the beach.

D By bus.

E A new skateboard.

F Because he's a great guitarist.

2 **Put the words in order to make questions.**

1 did / where / put her bag / Sara?

   Where did Sarah put her bag ?

2 arrive late / you / did / why?

   _____ ?

3 take last year / how many / exams / did / you?

   _____ ?

4 what / you / wear at the party / did?

   _____ ?

5 you / did / make this cake / how?

   _____ ?

6 did / go home / Kim / when?

   _____ ?

3 **Write questions about the past.**

1 My sister got up early. Why _did_ _she get up_ early?

2 My parents went out. Where _____ ?

3 Jenny phoned her mom. When _____ ?

4 Eric broke his leg. How _____ ?

5 Dad cooked a meal. What _____ ?

6 Darius bought some CDs. How many _____ ?

Unit 6

Vocabulary

1 Fill in the blanks with the correct adjectives.

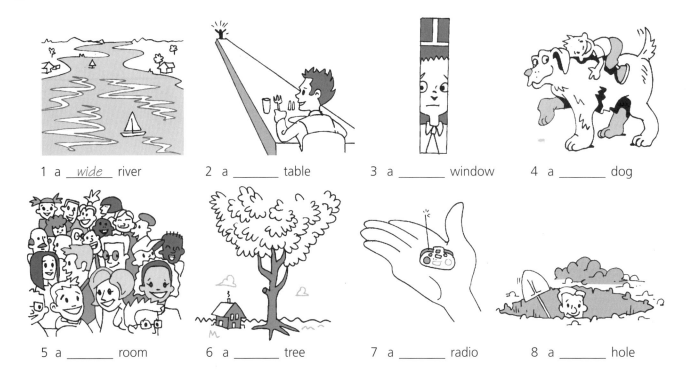

1 a _wide_ river

2 a _____ table

3 a _____ window

4 a _____ dog

5 a _____ room

6 a _____ tree

7 a _____ radio

8 a _____ hole

2 Fill in the blanks with the words below.

width length weight depth height length

1 The _length_ of a tennis court is about 23 meters.

2 The _____ of the net is about one meter.

3 The _____ of the ball is about 60 grams.

4 The _____ of an Olympic swimming pool is exactly 50 meters. The _____ is 25 meters.

5 The _____ of the water is at least 2 meters.

Extend your vocabulary

Grammar

1 Circle the correct form of the adjective.

1 That's the **deepest** / **most deep** swimming pool in the city.
2 She's the **helpfullest** / **most helpful** student in our class.
3 My brother is the **lazyest** / **laziest** person in our family.
4 This is **largest** / **the largest** house in the neighborhood.
5 Love Story is the **sadest** / **saddest** movie in the world!
6 This is the **cheapest** / **most cheap** DVD player in the store.

2 Fill in the blanks with the superlatives of the adjectives below.

> expensive   tall   fat   funny   bad   old

1 Bob is _the tallest_ student in our class.

2 *Comedy hour* is _____ program on TV!

3 Grandma is _____ person in our family.

4 I'm _____ player on our team!

5 That's _____ camera in the store.

6 Rex is _____ dog in our neighborhood!

3 Write sentences using the superlative.

1 Today is a hot day.
  It's _the hottest day_ of the year.

2 That's a wide river.
  It's _____ in the country.

3 Ron is a talkative boy.
  He's _____ in the class

4 That's a big building.
  It's _____ in the city.

5 Miss Jones is a young teacher
  She's _____ in the school.

6 "Rikki's" is a good club.
  It's _____ in town.

Vocabulary

1 Fill in the blanks with words from the wordsearch.

U	B	E	N	A	M	D	E
P	A	S	S	P	O	R	T
C	R	E	D	I	T	U	I
Q	G	L	E	V	O	L	C
C	A	M	P	L	U	E	K
L	I	T	T	E	R	S	E
Y	N	E	A	B	X	H	T

1 When you go on vacation, you have to carry your _____*passport*_____ .

2 Before you get on the bus, you have to buy a _____ .

3 You can't _____ in my garden!

4 If you want, you can take a _____ around the city.

5 When you're in school, you have to follow the _____ .

6 You can't drop _____ on the street!

7 Sorry, you can't use a _____ card here. You have to pay in cash.

8 This market is great! We can _____ for souvenirs here.

2 Label the pictures with words below.

> tent backpack hiking boots raincoat compass map

Hiking holidays in New Zealand

Equipment

We give you ...

1 *tent*

2 _____

3 _____

You have to bring ...

4 _____

5 _____

6 _____

Grammar

1 Circle the correct words.

1 It's late. We **have to** / **can't** hurry!

2 You **have to** / **can't** drive my car! You don't have a licence.

3 I want to be a doctor, so I **have to** / **can't** do well on my exams.

4 Kenny **has to** / **can't** come to the soccer match. He doesn't have a ticket.

5 You **have to** / **can't** be careful when you cross this road. There's a lot of traffic.

2 Fill in the gaps using *can* or *don't have to*.

1 You *don't have to* buy a bottle of soda. There's one in the refrigerator – you _____ drink it if you want.

2 There's a holiday today, so we _____ go to school. We _____ go to the beach!

3 The store is only a hundred meters away. We _____ walk there. We _____ get a taxi!

4 "Giovanni's" is a great restaurant, and it's cheap. You _____ eat a good meal there, and you _____ spend much money.

3 What do these signs mean? Fill in the blanks with *can*, *can't*, *have to* or *don't have to*.

1 You _____*have to*_____ turn left.

2 You _____ buy a drink here.

3 You _____ open this door!

4 You _____ show your passport here.

5 You _____ use the stairs. You can use the elevator!

6 You _____ turn left.

7 You _____ ask for information here.

8 You _____ pay to go on the bus.

Unit 7

Vocabulary

1 Match the pictures with the sentences below.

They're fighting. 5   She's hiding. ☐   They're arguing. ☐

She's shouting. ☐   He's hitting his brother. ☐

Extend your vocabulary

2 Label the pictures with the words below. Then fill in the blanks in the story.

witness   robber   judge   police officer

On Monday, a (1) ___robber___ stole $100,000 from the Central Bank. The next day, a (2) _____ arrested the robber. In court, a (3) _____ said "I saw him on Monday. He was running down the road with a bag full of money. He was holding a gun. He stole the money!"

The (4) _____ sent the robber to prison for ten years.

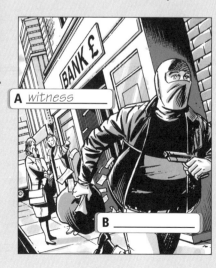

A _witness_

B _____

C _____

D _____

Grammar

1 Circle the correct word.

1 Roger **was** / **were** arguing with Alice at the party.

2 We **wasn't** / **weren't** waiting for a bus at 4:00. We **was** / **were** waiting for a taxi.

3 The sun **was** / **were** shining yesterday afternoon.

4 Martha **wasn't** / **weren't** watching a movie at 8:00. She **was** / **were** playing a computer game.

5 I **was** / **were** sleeping when you phoned last night.

6 Eric and Sven **was** / **were** playing CDs yesterday evening.

2 Look at the chart. Then complete the dialogs using the past progressive of the verbs in parentheses.

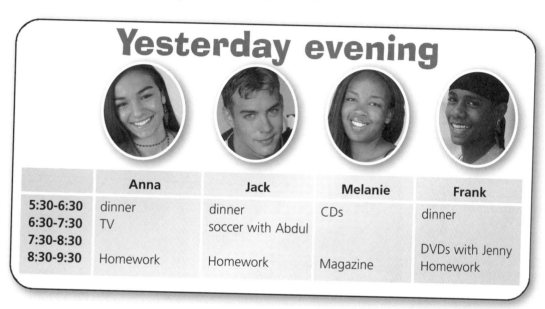

	Anna	Jack	Melanie	Frank
5:30-6:30	dinner	dinner	CDs	dinner
6:30-7:30	TV	soccer with Abdul		
7:30-8:30				DVDs with Jenny
8:30-9:30	Homework	Homework	Magazine	Homework

Melanie: (1) I _was doing_ (do) my homework at 6:00 yesterday evening.

Melanie's mom: That's not true! You (2) _____ (not / do) your homework.

                        You (3) _____ (listen) to CDs!

Anna: I (4) _____ (watch) TV at 7:00. What about you? Were you at home?

Jack: No, I wasn't. I was in the park with Abdul. We (5) _____ (play) soccer.

Frank's dad: Who was in your room at 8:00? It was noisy. Your radio was too loud!

Frank: I was with Jenny. We (6) _____ (not / listen) the radio.

                       We (7) _____ (watch) DVDs.

3 These sentences are wrong. Write the correct sentences.

1 Anna was having dinner at 7:00.

   She _wasn't having dinner_ . She _was watching_ TV.

2 Frank was sleeping at 9:00.

   He _____ . He _____ his homework.

3 Melanie was watching TV at 9:00.

   _____ . _____ .

4 Jack and Anna were doing their homework at 6:00.

   _____ . _____ .

Vocabulary

1 **Fill in the blanks with the words below.**

> garage   street corner   bank   fire escape   apartment   police station

1 Where were you? I was waiting on the _____*street corner*_____ but I didn't see you!
2 Quick! The building is burning! Run down the _____!
3 They arrested the robbers and took them to the _____.
4 You can keep your money in the _____.
5 When Tony gets home from work he leaves his car in the _____.
6 In cities, a lot of people live in an _____.

2 **These are some places you can find in the city. Label the pictures with the words below.**

> stadium   bus station   apartment building   parking lot   post office   library

1 ___*post office*___

2 _____

3 _____

4 _____

5 _____

6 _____

Extend your vocabulary

Grammar

1 Match the questions with the answers.

1 Hi, Dan. I saw you at the party. Were you enjoying it?

2 What were you doing yesterday evening?

3 Why was Layla carrying a suitcase?

4 Were you and Elena walking to the bus station?

5 Where was Sam going yesterday morning?

6 Were the children playing computer games?

A Because she was going to her grandma's for the weekend.

B He was going to the dentist.

C No, they weren't. They were listening to CDs.

D Yes, I was. It was great!

E I was watching a DVD with Nicky.

F No, we weren't. We were walking to the library.

2 Put the words in order to make questions.

1 at the party / was / she / what / wearing?
  What was she wearing at the party ?

2 running / why / this morning / you / were?
  _____ ?

3 they / where / going / at lunchtime / were?
  _____ ?

4 raining / it / was / yesterday morning?
  _____ ?

5 on Saturday / soccer / playing / were / they?
  _____ ?

6 he / was / doing / at 8:00 / what?
  _____ ?

3 Write questions about the party using *where*, *why* or *what*.

1 Fiona was shouting.
  Why _____was she_____ shouting?
  Because she was angry.

2 Pam and Dev were watching a movie.
  What _____ watching?
  They were watching *Star Wars*.

3 Jess and Paula were talking.
  Where _____ ?
  They were talking in the kitchen.

4 Marco was eating.
  _____ ?
  He was eating pizza.

5 Maggie and Pedro were dancing.
  _____ ?
  They were dancing in the garden.

6 Antonia was playing an instrument.
  _____ ?
  She was playing the guitar.

7 Carlos was sleeping.
  _____ ?
  Because he was very tired!

Unit 8

Vocabulary

1 Unscramble the words below and do the crossword.

1 zibalzdr
2 ireurchan
3 stofer efir
4 imustan
5 hilastrom
6 equarhaket
7 fodol
8 dorotan

2 Fill in the blanks with the words below.

dark calm light dry dangerous safe wet rough

Extend your vocabulary

1 We were traveling to an island. The sea wasn't _calm_.
It was ________!

3 The sky wasn't ________.
It was ________!

2 We weren't ________.
We were ________!

4 Finally, we arrived at the island. It was a ________ journey, but we were _safe_!

Grammar

1 Are these sentences about actions in progress or completed actions? Check (✔) one box for each sentence.

	Action in progress	Completed action
1 Angela dropped a glass.		✔
2 The children were sleeping.		
3 I was walking to school.		
4 Tommy heard a loud noise.		
5 Jackie passed her exam.		
6 We were watching TV yesterday evening.		
7 Marisa bought a new cell phone.		
8 Michael was practicing the piano.		

2 Circle the correct word.

1 Daisy **was** / were talking on the phone.
2 My parents were **cook** / **cooking** a meal.
3 I **opened** / **opening** the box, but it was empty.
4 Olga and Karen **wasn't** / **weren't** enjoying the party.

5 Tommy **doesn't** / **didn't** buy the laptop. It was too expensive.
6 Luis **wasn't** / **weren't** running very fast.

3 These sentences are wrong. Look at the pictures and write correct sentences.

1 Vincent and Tara were playing soccer. They _weren't playing_ soccer. They _were playing_ tennis.

2 Sandra broke her leg. She didn't _____ leg. She _____ her arm.

3 Mark's parents bought a new house. They didn't _____ _____. They _____ car.

4 Paul was waiting outside the movie theater. He wasn't _____ _____. _____.

5 Ed and Gill were eating candy. They _____ _____. _____ ice cream.

6 Cathy sent a postcard. _____ _____. _____ _____ e-mail.

Vocabulary

1 Circle the eight adverbs (→ or ↓) in the wordsearch. Then write the words.

D	A	C	L	Y	H	E	R	Q
E	J	H	Z	O	Y	N	S	U
Q	U	I	E	T	L	Y	X	I
P	T	W	T	H	A	R	D	C
A	N	G	R	I	L	Y	W	K
S	L	U	X	K	O	B	E	L
C	A	R	E	F	U	L	L	Y
N	C	L	O	E	D	I	L	N
H	A	P	P	I	L	Y	U	N
I	V	T	E	S	Y	K	D	E

1 a _ngrily_
2 q _____
3 w _____
4 h _____
5 c _____
6 h _____
7 l _____
8 q _____

2 Fill in the blanks with the words below.

> serious funny interesting valuable strange difficult

1 We love this comedy show. It's really ___funny___! 2 I like this story. It's _____.

3 I can't do this exam. It's _____! 4 Look at this ring. It's very _____.

5 Look at this picture. It's very _____! 6 There was an accident near my house yesterday. It was _____.

Extend your vocabulary

Grammar

1 Write the adverbs from these adjectives.

1 busy → _____busily_____
2 beautiful → _____
3 fast → _____

4 lazy → _____
5 strange → _____
6 easy → _____

2 Write sentences using adverbs.

1 She's a slow walker. She ____walks slowly____ .
2 They're hard workers. They _____ .
3 He's a bad swimmer. He _____ .

4 They're good players. They _____ .
5 We're quick learners. We _____ .
6 He's a fast driver. He _____ .

3 Circle the correct word.

1 The students were reading **quiet** / **quietly** in the library.
2 Mr Davies is a **good** / **well** teacher.
3 Terry is always **happy** / **happily**.
4 We were listening **careful** / **carefully**.
5 Dad doesn't like **loud** / **loudly** music.
6 I play the guitar very **bad** / **badly**!
7 My suitcase is **heavy** / **heavily**.
8 The crowd was shouting **angry** / **angrily**.

4 Fill in the blanks with the adverbs of the adjectives in parentheses.

I was sailing a boat in Tahiti when I heard news about a storm on the radio. I (1) ___quickly___ (quick) called the rescue team, but the radio didn't work (2) _____ (good). The storm was coming, so I sailed (3) _____ (careful).
I saw another boat passing by, so I shouted (4) _____ (loud). They didn't see me. Then I fell over and hit my head (5) _____ (hard). I woke up 27 hours later and got up (6) _____ (slow) because I felt weak. After 42 days I got to the coast and I survived.

Unit 9

Vocabulary

1 Fill in the blanks with the words below.

> spin   bend   hit   land   stretch   kick   jump   pass

1   Before you play any sport, you should warm up. You should __*bend*__ your knees, and _____ your arms and legs.

2   When you're ice-skating, you can _____ high, _____ in the air, then _____ again on the ice. But be careful – it can be dangerous. You should have some lessons first!

3   When you play soccer, you can _____ the ball, but you can't _____ it with your hands. You can _____ the ball to other players.

2 Label the photos with the words below.

> net   bat   goggles   racket   ball   helmet   goalposts   club

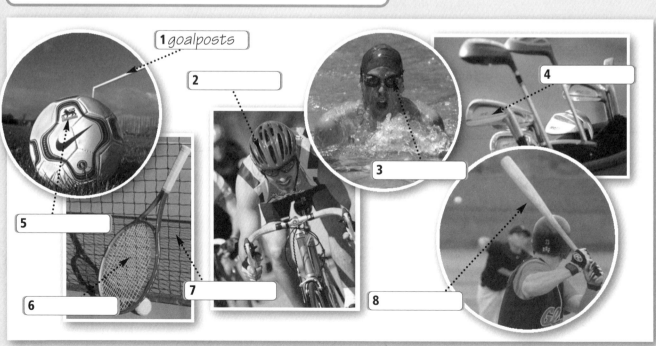

1 *goalposts*

2 _____

3 _____

4 _____

5 _____

6 _____

7 _____

8 _____

Extend your vocabulary

Grammar

1 **Fill in the blanks with *should* or *shouldn't*.**

1 A: Ruby has a toothache. Should she visit the doctor?

   B: No, she ____*shouldn't*____ . She _____ visit the dentist!

2 Those students _____ walk on the road. It's dangerous! They _____ stay on the sidewalk.

3 Timmy _____ go out in a T-shirt. It's cold and rainy. He _____ wear a coat!

4 A: Grandpa has a terrible cough. _____ he stop smoking?

   B: Yes, he _____ !

2 **Put the words in order to make sentences.**

1 should / early / you / go to bed

   You should go to bed early _____ .

2 a lot of coffee / people / drink / shouldn't

   _____ .

3 students / every evening / do their homework / should

   _____ .

4 every day / shouldn't / you / eat fast food

   _____ .

5 visit the dentist / children / should / twice a year

   _____ .

6 shouldn't / work / all the time / you

   _____ .

3 **Complete the dialogs. Write questions and answers using should and the words in parentheses.**

1 A: I can't read magazines or newspapers. The writing is too small! ____*What should I do*____? (what / I / do)

   B: Maybe you need glasses. _____ . (you / visit / the optician)

2 A: Richard is tired all the time. He doesn't have any energy. _____? (what / he / do)

   B: _____ . (exercise more) Cycling and swimming are good.

3 A: My friend and I want to visit Iceland. _____? (when / we / go)

   B: _____ .(go / in the summer) Don't go in the winter – it's freezing!

4 A: Anna is new to this town. She wants to meet people. _____? (where / she / go)

   B: _____ . (go / to the youth club) A lot of teenagers go there.

Vocabulary

1 **Find the sports in the word snake. Then write the words below.**

tracklacrossebasketballhorsebackridingwaterskiingkarategolf

1 You do this sport on two wheels. _cycling_

2 You do this sport on a lake or on the sea. _____

3 You use a special stick with a net to play this sport. _____

4 You have to be good at catching, running and throwing to play this sport. _____

5 You need clubs and a ball to play this sport, and you play it on a very big course. _____

6 You do this sport on four legs. _____

7 This sport includes the high jump, the long jump and the 100 meters race. _____

8 You don't need any equipment to do this sport – you use your hands and feet! _____

2 **Fill in the blanks with the words below.**

miss   drop   throw   bounce   roll   save

1 Don't _drop_ the ball!

2 Don't _____ the goal!

3 In baseball, you have to _____ the ball.

4 The goalkeeper has to _____ goals.

5 In bowling, you have to _____ the ball.

6 In basketball, you can _____ the ball.

Extend your vocabulary

Grammar

	Anita	David	Linda and Eric
Monday	go swimming		sunbathe
Tuesday	play tennis	play soccer	visit Aunt Jane
Wednesday	do karate	watch a baseball game	drive to the shopping mall
Thursday	go climbing	go swimming	watch movies
Friday	take photos	buy a new skateboard	have dinner at a restaurant
Saturday	have a party		play golf
Sunday	fly home!		

1 **Look at the chart. Who is saying these sentences?**

1 "I'm going to buy a new skateboard on Friday."
   ___David___

2 "We're going to have a party on Saturday!"
   _____ and _____

3 "My brother's going to watch a baseball game on Wednesday." _____

4 "I'm going to go swimming on Thursday."
   _____

5 "We're going to play golf on Saturday."
   _____ and _____

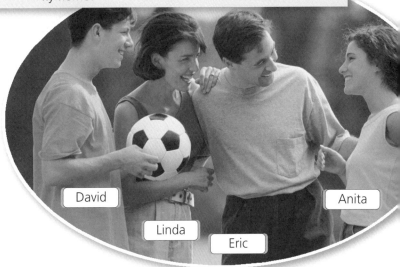

David   Linda   Eric   Anita

2 **Write questions about Anita and her family using the words in parentheses.**

1 _____What is Anita going to do_____
   on Tuesday? (What / Anita / do)
   She's going to play tennis.

2 _____
   on Monday? (What / Anita and David / do)
   They're going to go swimming.

3 _____
   on Friday? (What / David / buy)
   He's going to buy a new skateboard.

4 _____
   home? (When / they / fly)
   They're going to fly home on Sunday.

5 _____
   on Wednesday? (Anita / do karate)
   Yes, she is.

6 _____
   on Tuesday? (Linda and Eric / play soccer)
   No, they aren't.

3 **You are talking to Anita. Complete the dialog.**

You: (1) _Are you going to_ go climbing on your vacation?

Anita: Yes. I'm (2) _____going to_____ go climbing on Thursday. But my brother doesn't like climbing. He's (3) _____ swimming.

You: (4) _____ to visit Aunt Jane on your vacation?

Anita: No, (5) _____. But Mom and Dad (6) _____ visit her on Tuesday.

You: When (7) _____ come home?

Anita: We're (8) _____ fly home on Sunday.

You: Have a great time!

Anita: Thanks. (9) _____ enjoy our vacation!

Unit 10

Vocabulary

1 **Unscramble the verbs. Then do the crossword.**

1 When you swim in the sea, you can ___float___ (tafol) on the water.

2 Don't _____ (pord) that bottle!

3 Next year I'm going to _____ (blimc) a mountain.

4 When you play basketball, you have to _____ (ebucon) the ball on the ground.

5 Don't _____ (pmub) into the wall – it's hard!

6 Don't keep the ball – _____ (whotr) it to your teammate.

7 The ball's coming to you – _____ (chact) it!

8 The water in this swimming pool is very warm. _____ (evdi) in!

Extend your vocabulary

2 **Fill in the blanks with the words below.**

push   carry   pull   lift   turn

1 He's ___lift___ing the box.

2 They're _____ing the table.

3 He's _____ing the sofa.

4 He's _____ing the sofa.

5 He's _____ing the key.

Grammar

1 Put the words in order to make predictions.

In ten years' time …

1 won't / I / with my parents / live
  I won't live with my parents .

2 a house / buy / I / will
  _____ .

3 be / Sue / a student / won't
  _____ .

4 will / she / in the city / work
  _____ .

5 a bicycle / I / ride / won't
  _____ .

6 drive a car / will / I
  _____ .

7 money / give me / won't / my parents
  _____ .

8 I / have / a job / will
  _____ .

2 These sentences about the future are incomplete. Ask questions about the missing information.

In the year 2050 …

1 People will go on vacation to xxx. _Where will people go on vacation_ ?
2 We will travel by xxx. How _____ ?
3 Students will wear xxx. What _____ ?
4 xxx will build houses. Who _____ ?
5 We will start school at xxx. What time _____ ?
6 There will be xxx TV channels. How many _____ ?
7 Schools will be xxx. What _____ like?

3 Joe and Jim are talking about the future. Fill in the blanks with _will_ or _won't_ and the verbs in parentheses.

Joe: How old (1) _will you be_ (you / be) in 20 years' time?

Jim: (2) ____I'll be____ (I / be) 35. Wow!

Joe: (3) _____ (you / be) a teacher?

Jim: No, I (4) _____ . I'll be a musician. Maybe a guitarist.

Joe: (5) _____ (you / have) a lot of money?

Jim: I don't know. I think (6) _____ (I / have) enough money.

Joe: (7) _____ (you / have) any children?

Jim: Yes, I (8) _____ . I'll marry a beautiful girl, and (9) _____ (we / have) two children. (10) _____ (they / be) very intelligent, like me!

Joe: Where (11) _____ (you / live)?

Jim: (12) _____ (we / not / live) in the city. (13) _____ (we / have) a nice house in the country. (14) _____ (there / be) fields and woods around the house.

Vocabulary

1 Match the adjectives with the pictures below. Then write the opposites. Use the words below.

far   cold   dangerous   unstable   close   wet   stable   safe   warm   dry

1 _unstable_ _____   2 _____ _____   3 _____ _____

4 _____ _____   5 _____ _safe_

2 Look at the picture. Fill in the blanks with the words below.

volcanoes   clouds   mountains   lightning   valleys

Will it be possible to live on Venus? Probably not!

There are tall (1) _mountains_ and deep (2) _____. There are a lot of (3) _____, too. The atmosphere is poisonous, and there are thick (4) _____ in the sky. There isn't any rain, but there's (5) _____ all the time. It's hot – the average temperature is about 400°C. It's a dangerous place!

Extend your vocabulary

Grammar

1 Circle the correct words.

1 I can't understand this book. It's (too difficult) / not difficult enough.
2 Emma runs slowly. She won't win the race. She's **too fast** / **not fast enough**.
3 This coffee is burning my mouth. It's **too hot** / **not hot enough**.
4 Tim's only 14 years old. He can't drive a car. He's **too young** / **not young enough**.
5 We can't walk to the shopping mall. It's **too close** / **not close enough**.

2 Write sentences using *too* and the adjectives below.

> heavy   wide   dangerous   expensive

1 There are snakes in that room. Don't go in. It's *too dangerous* !
2 We can't swim across the river. It's _____ .
3 That watch costs $1,000. I can't buy it. It's _____ .
4 I can't lift this table. It's _____ .

3 Write sentences using *not enough* and the adjectives below.

> big   warm   good   quiet

1 I don't want to go to the beach today. It isn't _____ *warm enough* _____ .
2 We can't put all these suitcases in the car. It isn't _____ .
3 I can't study in this room. Everyone's talking. It isn't _____ .
4 I play soccer badly. I want to be on the team, but I'm _____ .

4 Write sentences about these people using *too* or *not enough* and the adjectives in parentheses. These people can't be lifeguards. Why not?

1 Sheila is 1.55m tall. (tall)
She *isn't tall enough* .

2 Harry is 59. (old)
_____ .

3 Val weighs 55 kg. (heavy)
_____ .

4 Ricky is 14. (old)
_____ .

5 Guy weighs 95 kg. (heavy)
_____ .

6 Theo can swim at 3 km/h. (fast)
_____ .

Unit 11

Vocabulary

1 Complete the puzzle using the words below.

> hairstylist   dance   bodyguard   artist   stylist   coach

1 The _____ teacher helps you to move well.
2 The acting _____ helps you to act better.
3 The _____ cuts your hair.
4 The _____ keeps you safe.
5 The makeup _____ can change your face.
6 The _____ chooses the best clothes.

	¹d	a	n	c	e		
		²					
³							
			⁴				
			⁵				
			⁶				

What's the mystery word? They work with _____

2 Label the picture with the words below.

> stage   microphone   camera   audience   screens   lights

1 audience
2 _____
3 _____
4 _____
5 _____
6 _____

Grammar

1 **Look at the chart about plans for tomorrow. Answer the questions about Erika and Phil using short answers.**

Erika
Tomorrow
go to the dentist 9:30
play tennis 10:00
have lunch with Karen
have piano lesson 4:00
evening - go to rock concert
with Brian

Phil
Tomorrow
morning – play soccer
meet Maria at the café 1:00
go to the doctor 3:00
7:00 – have dinner with Charlie
go to movies with Alison 8:30

Erika

Phil

1 Is Erika having a guitar lesson at 4:00 tomorrow? _No, she isn't_ .

2 Is Phil playing soccer tomorrow morning? _____.

3 Are Phil and Charlie having dinner at 6:00? _____.

4 Is Erika playing tennis at 10:00? _____.

5 Are Erika and Brian going to a rock concert in the evening? _____.

6 Is Phil going to the dentist at 3:00? _____.

2 **These sentences are wrong. Write correct sentences (negative and affirmative) about tomorrow.**

1 Erika is having lunch with Martha.
   She isn't _____having lunch with Martha_____. She's _____having lunch_____ with Karen.

2 Phil is meeting Maria at the library.
   He isn't _____. He's _____ at the café.

3 Erika and Brian are going to a rock concert in the morning.
   They _____. _____.

4 Erika is seeing the dentist at 10:30.
   _____. _____.

5 Phil and Alison are going to the movies at 7:00.
   _____. _____.

3 **Complete the dialog between Erika and Phil using the verbs in parentheses. Use the present progressive.**

Phil: Hi, Erika. (1) _Are you playing tennis_ tomorrow? (you / play)

Erika: Yes, I am. But (2) _____ the dentist first. (I / see)

Phil: Really? What time (3) _____ the dentist? (you / see)

Erika: At 9:30. What about you? What (4) _____ tomorrow? (you / do)

Phil: (5) _____ soccer in the morning. (I / play) In the evening, (6) _____ to the movies. (I / go)

Erika: (7) _____ with you? (Alison / go)

Phil: Yes, she is. Come with us!

Erika: I can't. (8) _____ Brian in the evening. (I / meet)
       (9) _____ to a rock concert! (we / go)

Vocabulary

1 Find eight words about health problems in the wordsearch. Then write the words.

O	L	C	E	T	R	I	T	H
T	O	O	T	H	A	C	H	E
S	Y	L	A	R	L	R	E	B
U	N	D	Z	O	T	Y	A	N
N	I	O	M	A	V	T	D	E
B	L	I	S	T	E	R	A	Q
U	C	R	T	E	K	S	C	O
R	P	I	M	P	L	E	H	Z
N	E	C	A	N	K	L	E	R

1 sprained a *nkle*   2 b_____   3 h_____   4 t_____

5 sore t_____   6 p_____   7 s_____   8 c_____

2 Label the pictures with the words below.

nurse   paramedic   doctor   surgeon   ambulance driver   lab technician

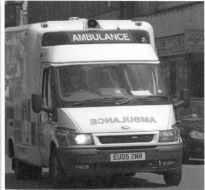

1 _____*doctor*_____   2 _____   3 _____

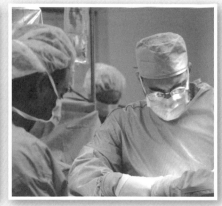

4 _____   5 _____   6 _____

Grammar

1 Match the problems with the offers.

1 I have a headache.
2 I can't read this newspaper.
3 I'm thirsty.
4 My train leaves in five minutes.
5 I'm hungry.
6 I don't understand this homework.

A I'll buy you a soda.
B I'll explain it to you.
C I'll make a pizza.
D I'll get you an aspirin.
E I'll take you to the station.
F I'll get your glasses.

2 Write offers using *I'll* or *We'll* and the phrases below.

carry it for you   fix it   push it for you   pick it up   open the door

1 We'll push it for you.

3 Write offers using the words below.

cook   take you   shut   buy you   make

1 Your friend wants to go to a concert with you, but she doesn't have a ticket, and she doesn't have any money!

   I'll buy you a ticket .

2 Everyone in your family is hungry. They want their dinner! Your mom doesn't have time to cook.

   _____ the dinner.

3 It's your friend's birthday tomorrow, and you want to celebrate. You are good at making cakes.

   _____ .

4 It's wet and windy outside. The window is open, and everyone in the room is cold.

   _____ the window.

5 Your friend has a terrible toothache. He wants to go to the dentist, but it's too far to walk. You have a car.

   _____ .

Unit 12

Vocabulary

1 Unscramble the words.

Do you want to change your appearance?

You can ...

1 have a (otatot) _tattoo_

2 have a (cipering) ....

3 (yed) .... your hair

Do you want to try an extreme sport?

You can ...

4 go (drawsnoobing) ....

5 go (kysviding) ....

6 go (enbuge) .... jumping

7 go (achuparting) ....

Do you want to meet new people?

You can ...

8 go on a (dinlb)

....

date

2 Label the pictures with the words below.

rowboat   mountain bike   speedboat   sports car   scooter   hang glider

1 _____mountain bike_____   2 _____   3 _____
4 _____   5 _____   6 _____

Grammar

1 Write the past participles of these regular and irregular verbs.

Regular		Irregular	
1 play → _played_		6 do → _done_	
2 paint → _____		7 meet → _____	
3 watch → _____		8 ride → _____	
4 travel → _____		9 write → _____	
5 climb → _____		10 eat → _____	

2 Look at the chart about the experiences of four students.

Dan

Sally

Marco

Nicola

	Dan	Sally	Marco	Nicola
horse?	yes	yes	never	never
Japanese food?	never	yes	never	yes
speedboat?	never	never	yes	yes
basketball?	yes	never	yes	never
bungee jumping?	yes	never	never	yes
mountain?	never	yes	yes	never

3 Look at the chart. Circle the correct verb.

1 Dan and Nicola **has** /**have** been bungee jumping.
2 Marco **has** / **have** never eaten Japanese food.
3 Marco and Nicola **has** / **have** never ridden a horse.
4 Sally **has** / **have** climbed a mountain.
5 Dan and Marco **has** / **have** played basketball.

4 Look at the chart again. Then complete the sentences about the students' experiences. Use the correct form of the verbs in parentheses.

1 Marco has _____climbed_____ a mountain. (climb)
2 Dan and Sally have never _____ in a speedboat. (travel)
3 Dan and Sally _____ a horse. (ride)
4 Sally and Marco _____ bungee jumping. (go)
5 Nicola _____ basketball. (play)
6 Sally _____ Japanese food. (eat)

Vocabulary

1 Find eight verbs in this word snake. Then write the words.

1 f_all_ _over_
2 s_____ _____
3 b_____
4 b_____ _____
5 t_____
6 w_____
7 f_____ _____
8 s_____

Write the sentence hidden in the word snake:

Have _____ _____ _____ _____ _____ ?

2 Complete the chart with the verbs and past participles. Use the words below.

> feel   smelled   taste   hear   seen   tasted   felt   smell   see   heard

The five senses

  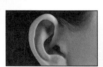

verb	1 _see_	2 _____	3 _____	4 _____	5 _____
participle	6 _____	7 _____	8 _____	9 _smelled_	10 _____

3 Fill in the blanks with the correct past participle from exercise 2.

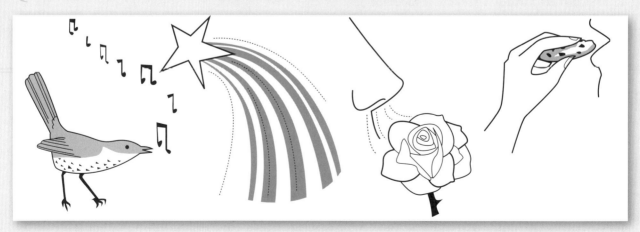

1 Have you ever ___heard___ birdsong?   2   Have you ever _____ a shooting star?
3 Have you ever _____ a rose?   4   Have you ever _____ my mom's cookies?

Grammar

1 Put the words in order to make questions.

1 you / have / fallen asleep / in class / ever?
   Have you ever fallen asleep in class ?

2 a motorbike / has / your teacher / ridden / ever?
   _____ ?

3 ever / visited / your friends / an art gallery / have?
   _____ ?

4 your parents / have / snowboarding / ever / been?
   _____ ?

5 broken / ever / have / a window / you?
   _____ ?

6 your dog / on your bed / slept / ever / has?
   _____ ?

2 Look at the chart. Then write short answers.

	Rita	Carlos	Amanda
travel?	I've visited France.	I've visited Spain and England.	I've visited France and Brazil.
music?	I've played the guitar and the piano.	I've played the guitar.	I've played the violin.
unusual sports?	I've been surfing.	I've been snowboarding.	I've been surfing and skydiving.
unusual transport?	I've ridden a motorbike.	I've ridden a horse and a camel.	I've ridden a horse.

1 Has Rita ever been snowboarding? _No, she hasn't_ .

2 Has Carlos ever played the guitar? _____ .

3 Have Rita and Amanda ever visited England? _____ .

4 Has Amanda ever played the violin? _____ .

5 Have Carlos and Amanda ever ridden a horse? _____ .

6 Has Carlos ever ridden a motorbike? _____ .

3 Look at the chart again. You are talking to Rita. Complete the dialog using the verbs in parentheses.

You: (1) Have _____ _you ever visited_ _____ England? (you / visit)

Rita: No, I haven't.

You: What about Carlos? Has (2) _____ England? (he / visit)

Rita: Yes, (3) _____ . He's been to Spain, too.

You: (4) _____ a motorbike? (Carlos and Amanda / ride)

Rita: (5) _____ , they _____ .

You: (6) _____ the guitar? (you / play)

Rita: Yes, I (7) _____ . But I'm not very good!

You: What about Amanda? (8) _____ the guitar? (she / play)

Rita: (9) _____ . But she's played the violin. It's difficult!

The Phantom of the Opera

'Quick! Quick! Close the door! It's him!' Annie Sorelli ran into the dressing-room, her face white.

One of the girls ran and closed the door, and then they all turned to Annie Sorelli.

'Who? Where? What's the matter?' they cried.

'It's the ghost!' Annie said. 'In the passage. I saw him. He came through the wall in front of me! And ... and I saw his face!'

Most of the girls were afraid, but one of them, a tall girl with black hair, laughed.

'Pooh!' she said. 'Everybody says they see the Opera ghost, but there isn't really a ghost. You saw a shadow on the wall.' But she did not open the door, or look into the passage.

'Lots of people see him,' a second girl said. 'Joseph Buquet saw him two days ago. Don't you remember?'

Then all the girls began to talk at once.

'Joseph says the ghost is tall and he wears a black evening coat.'

'He has the head of a dead man, with a yellow face and no nose

'... And no eyes – only black holes!'

Then little Meg Giry spoke for the first time. 'Don't talk about him. He doesn't like it. My mother told me.'

'Your mother?' the girl with black hair said. 'What does your mother know about the ghost?'

'She says that Joseph Buquet is a fool. The ghost doesn't like people talking about him, and one day Joseph Buquet is going to be sorry, very sorry.'

'But what does your mother know? Tell us, tell us!' all the girls cried.

'Oh dear!' said Meg. 'But please don't say a word to anyone. You know my mother is the doorkeeper for some of the boxes in the Opera House. Well, Box 5 is the ghost's box! He watches the operas from that box, and sometimes he leaves flowers for my mother!'

'The ghost has a box! And leaves flowers in it!'

'Oh, Meg, your mother's telling you stories! How can the ghost have a box?'

'It's true, it's true, I tell you!' Meg said. 'Nobody buys tickets for Box 5, but the ghost always comes to it on opera nights.'

'So somebody does come there?'

'Why, no! ... The ghost comes, but there is nobody there.'

The dancers looked at Meg. 'But how does your mother know?' one of them asked.

'There's no man in a black evening coat, with a yellow face. That's all wrong. My mother never sees the ghost in Box 5, but she hears him! He talks to her, but there is nobody there! And he doesn't like people talking about him!'

But that evening the dancers could not stop talking about the Opera ghost. They talked before the opera, all through the opera, and after the opera. But they talked very quietly, and they looked behind them before they spoke.

When the opera finished, the girls went back to their dressing-room. Suddenly, they heard somebody in the passage, and Madame Giry, Meg's mother, ran into the room. She was a fat, motherly woman, with a red, happy face. But tonight her face was white.

'Oh girls.' she cried. 'Joseph Buquet is dead! You know he works a long way down, on the fourth floor under the stage. The other stage workers found his dead body there an hour ago – with a rope around his neck!'

'It's the ghost!' cried Meg Giry. 'The ghost killed him!'

1 Circle the correct answer.

1 Meg Giry and Annie Sorelli are **dancers** / **singers** at the Opera House.

2 Madame Giry is **a dancer** / **a doorkeeper**.

3 Madame Giry has **seen** / **heard** the ghost.

2 Fill in the blanks with the words below.

> the stage   the passage
> the dressing room   Box 5

1 Annie Sorelli saw the ghost in _the passage_.

2 The ghost watches the operas from _____.

3 Madame Giry talked to the dancers in

   _____.

4 Joseph Buquet worked under _____.

3 What do you think about the ghost? Check (✔) one sentence.

1 He was an opera singer who died a long time ago. ☐

2 He was Madame Giry's husband, and he died last year. ☐

3 He is not really a ghost – he is a man who is still alive. ☐

Extra reading 2

OXFORD BOOKWORMS LIBRARY
1

The Wizard of Oz

Dorothy lived in a small house in Kansas, with Uncle Henry, Aunt Em, and a little black dog called Toto.

There were no trees and no hills in Kansas, and it was often very windy. Sometimes the wind came very fast and very suddenly. That was a cyclone, and it could blow trees and people and buildings away. There were cellars under all the houses. And when a cyclone came, people went down into their cellars and stayed there.

One day Uncle Henry came out and looked up at the sky. Then he ran quickly back into the house.

'There's a cyclone coming,' he called to Aunt Em and Dorothy. 'We must go down into the cellar!'

They ran to the door of the cellar, but Toto was afraid, and he ran under the bed. Dorothy ran after him.

'Quick!' shouted Aunt Em from the cellar. 'Leave the dog and come down into the cellar!'

Dorothy picked up Toto and ran to the cellar door. But before she got there, the cyclone hit the house.

And then a very strange thing happened.

The house moved, and then it went slowly up, up, up into the sky. Aunt Em and Uncle Henry were down in the cellar under the ground, but the house, Dorothy, and Toto went up to the top of the cyclone. Dorothy looked through the open cellar door and saw hills and houses, a long way down. She closed the cellar door quickly.

The wind blew the house along for many hours. At first Dorothy was afraid.

'But we can't do anything about it,' she said to Toto. 'So let's wait and see.' And after two or three hours, she and Toto went to sleep.

When Dorothy opened her eyes again, the house was on the ground and everything was quiet. She picked up Toto, opened the door, and went out. They saw tall trees and beautiful flowers, and little houses with blue doors.

Dorothy gave a little cry. 'This isn't Kansas, Toto! And who are these people?'

There were three very short men in blue hats, coats and trousers, and a little old woman in a beautiful white dress. The woman walked up to Dorothy and said, 'Thank you, thank you! Now the people are free!'

'Why are you thanking me?' Dorothy asked.

'You killed the Witch of the East,' said the woman. 'She was a bad witch, and her people, the Munchkins, were very afraid of her. Now she is dead, and we and the Munchkins want to thank you.'

The little old woman and the three little men all smiled happily at Dorothy, but Dorothy did not understand.

'But I didn't kill anybody!' she said.

'Your house fell on the Witch,' laughed the little woman. 'Look! You can see her feet!'

1 Fill in the blanks in the summary with the words below.

> dog   house   uncle   cellar   cyclone   bed

One day in Kansas, a (1) _cyclone_ hit Dorothy's house. Her (2) _____ and aunt went down into the (3) _____. Dorothy didn't go with them. She went to get her (4) _____ Toto, who was hiding under the (5) _____.
Suddenly the wind blew the (6) _____ into the air and carried it a long way.

2 Circle T (True) or F (False).

1 The house fell to the ground in Kansas. T / **F**
2 The house fell on the Witch of the East and killed her. T / F
3 The Munchkins were angry with Dorothy. T / F

3 What do you think will happen to Dorothy? Check (✔) Yes or No for each sentence.

	Yes	No
1 She will be Queen of the Munchkins.	☐	☐
2 She will go back to Kansas.	☐	☐
3 She will travel to another planet.	☐	☐

Extra reading 3

Robinson Crusoe

Before I begin my story, I would like to tell you a little about myself.

I was born in the year 1632, in the city of York in the north of England. My father was German, but he came to live and work in England. Soon after that, he married my mother, who was English. Her family name was Robinson, so, when I was born, they called me Robinson, after her.

My father did well in his business and I went to a good school. He wanted me to get a good job and live a quiet, comfortable life. But I didn't want that. I wanted adventure and an exciting life.

'I want to be a sailor and go to sea,' I told my mother and father. They were very unhappy about this.

'Please don't go,' my father said. 'You won't be happy, you know. Sailors have a difficult and dangerous life.' And because I loved him, and he was unhappy, I tried to forget about the sea.

But I couldn't forget, and about a year later, I saw a friend in town. His father had a ship, and my friend said to me, 'We're sailing to London tomorrow. Why don't you come with us?'

And so, on September 1st, 1651, I went to Hull, and the next day we sailed for London.

But, a few days later, there was a strong wind. The sea was rough and dangerous, and the ship went up and down, up and down. I was very ill, and very afraid.

'Oh, I don't want to die!' I cried. 'I want to live! If I live, I'll go home and never go to sea again!'

The next day the wind dropped, and the sea was quiet and beautiful again.

'Well, Bob,' my friend laughed. 'How do you feel now? The wind wasn't too bad.'

'What!' I cried. 'It was a terrible storm.'

'Oh, that wasn't a storm,' my friend answered. 'Just a little wind. Forget it. Come and have a drink.'

After a few drinks with my friend, I felt better. I forgot about the danger and decided not to go home. I didn't want my friends and family to laugh at me!

I stayed in London for some time, but I still wanted to go to sea. So, when the captain of a ship asked me to go with him to Guinea in Africa, I agreed. And so I went to sea for the second time.

It was a good ship and everything went well at first, but I was very ill again. Then, when we were near the Canary Islands, a Turkish pirate ship came after us. They were famous thieves of the sea at that time. There was a long, hard fight, but when it finished, we and the ship were prisoners.

The Turkish captain and his men took us to Sallee in Morocco. They wanted to sell us as slaves in the markets there. But in the end the Turkish captain decided to keep me for himself, and took me home with him. This was a sudden and terrible change in my life. I was now a slave and this Turkish captain was my master.

1 Circle T (True) or F (False).

1 Robinson Crusoe was born in England. T / F
2 Robinson Crusoe wanted a quiet, comfortable life. T / F
3 Robinson Crusoe enjoyed sailing in rough weather. T / F

2 Fill in the blanks in the summary with the words below.

> Morocco   Turkey   Hull   Guinea

Robinson Crusoe's first sea journey was from (1) __Hull__ to London. Then a ship's captain asked Robinson Crusoe to go with him to (2) _____, in Africa. But they had a fight with a pirate ship. The pirates' captain was from (3) _____. He took Robinson Crusoe and the other prisoners to (4) _____.

3 What do you think will happen to Robinson Crusoe? Check (✔) Yes or No for each sentence.

		Yes	No
1	He will escape from his Turkish master.	☐	☐
2	He will marry a Moroccan woman.	☐	☐
3	He will go back to England.	☐	☐

Extra reading 4

Anne of Green Gables

Matthew Cuthbert lived with his sister Marilla on their farm on Prince Edward Island in Canada. Their farmhouse, Green Gables, was just outside the little village of Avonlea. Matthew was nearly sixty and had a long brown beard. His sister was five years younger. They were both tall and thin, with dark hair. Everybody in Avonlea knew that the Cuthberts were quiet people who worked very hard on their farm.

One afternoon Matthew drove the horse and cart to the station. 'Has the five-thirty train arrived yet?' he asked the station-master.

'Yes,' the man replied. 'And there's a passenger who's waiting for you. A little girl.'

'A little girl?' asked Matthew. 'But I've come for a boy! The children's home is sending us one of their orphan boys. We're going to adopt him, you see, and he's going to help me with the farm work.'

'Well, perhaps the children's home didn't have any boys, so they sent you a girl,' answered the stationmaster carelessly. 'Here she is.'

Matthew turned shyly to speak to the child. She was about eleven, with long red hair in two plaits. Her face was small, white and thin, with a lot of freckles, and she had large grey-green eyes. She was wearing an old brown hat and a dress which was too small for her.

'Are you Mr Cuthbert of Green Gables?' she asked excitedly in a high, sweet voice. 'I'm very happy to come and live with you, and belong to you. I've never belonged to anyone, you see. The people at the children's home were very kind, but it's not very exciting to live in a place like that, is it?'

Matthew felt sorry for the child. How could he tell her that it was all a mistake? But he couldn't just leave her at the station. He decided to take her home with him. Marilla could explain the mistake to her.

He was surprised that he enjoyed the journey home. He was a quiet, shy man, and he didn't like talking himself. But today, he only had to listen, because the little girl talked and talked and talked. She told him all about herself while they drove along.

'My parents died when I was a baby, you know, and for the last three years I've had to work for my food. I've lived with three different families and looked after their children. So I've always been poor, and I haven't got any nice dresses! But I just imagine that I'm wearing the most beautiful blue dress, and a big hat with flowers on, and blue shoes, and then I'm happy! Do you imagine things sometimes?'

'Well, I . . . I . . . not often,' said Matthew.

They were now driving past some very old apple trees next to the road. The trees were full of sweet-smelling, snowy-white flowers. The little girl looked at them.

'Aren't the trees beautiful?' she said happily. 'But am I talking too much? Please tell me. I can stop if necessary, you know.'

Matthew smiled at her. 'You go on talking,' he answered. 'I like listening to you.'

'They sent you a girl,' said the station-master.

When they arrived at Green Gables, Marilla came to the door to meet them. But when she saw the little girl, she cried in surprise, 'Matthew, who's that? Where's the boy?'

'The children's home has made a mistake,' he said unhappily, 'and sent a girl, not a boy.'

The child was listening carefully. Suddenly she put her head in her hands and began to cry.

'You _ you don't want me!' she sobbed. 'Oh _ oh! You don't want me because I'm not a boy!'

'Now, now, don't cry,' said Marilla kindly.

'Don't you understand? Oh! This is the worst thing that's happened to me in all my life!'

'Well, you can stay here, just for tonight,' said Marilla. 'Now, what's your name?'

The child stopped crying. 'Will you please call me Cordelia?' she asked.

'Call you Cordelia? Is that your name?'

'Well, no, it isn't, but it's a very beautiful name, isn't it? I like to imagine my name is Cordelia, because my real name is Anne Shirley _ and that's not a very interesting name, is it?'

Marilla shook her head. 'The child has too much imagination,' she thought.

Later, when Anne was in bed, Marilla said to her brother, 'She must go back to the children's home tomorrow.'

'Marilla, don't you think . . .' began Matthew. 'She's a nice little thing, you know.'

'Matthew Cuthbert, are you telling me that you want to keep her?' asked Marilla crossly.

Matthew looked uncomfortable. 'Well, she's clever, and interesting, and —'

'But we don't need a girl!'

'But perhaps she needs us,' Matthew replied, surprisingly quickly for him. 'She's had a very unhappy life up to now, Marilla. She can help you in the house. I can get a boy from the village to help me on the farm. What do you think?'

Marilla thought for a long time. 'All right,' she said in the end, 'I agree. The poor child can stay. I'll look after her.'

Matthew smiled happily. 'Be as good and kind to her as you can, Marilla. I think she needs a lot of love.'

1 Who says these sentences? Match the sentences with the people.

1 Perhaps the children's home didn't have any boys, so they sent you a girl. _c_

2 I've lived with three different families and looked after their children. ____

3 Well, you can stay here, just for tonight. ____

4 She's a nice little thing, you know. ____

a Matthew Cuthbert

b Marilla Cuthbert

c the station-master

d Anne Shirley

2 Circle T (True) or F (False).

1 Anne has long, black hair. T / F

2 Anne is excited about coming to Green Gables. T / F

3 Matthew is a talkative man. T / F

4 Anne can help Marilla in the house. T / F

3 What do you think will happen to Anne in the story? Check (✔) Yes or No.

	Yes	No
1 She will go back to the children's home.	☐	☐
2 She will study to be a teacher.	☐	☐
3 She will marry a boy from the village.	☐	☐